Bavarian Crochet on-the-Go™

Contents

Hot Pads

SKILL LEVEL

INTERMEDIATE

FINISHED SIZE

9½ inches x 9½ inches

MATERIALS

- Omega Sinfonia light (light worsted) weight yarn (3½ oz/218 yds/100g per ball):
  1 ball each #821 mandarin (A), #802 cream (B), #883 coral (C) and #834 gold (D)
  Or
  1 ball each #879 purple (A), #883 coral (B), #802 cream (C) and #828 lilac (D)
- Size F/5/3.75mm crochet hook or size needed to obtain gauge
- Tapestry needle

GAUGE

2 shells and 3 sc = 4 inches

Take time to check gauge.

PATTERN NOTES

Weave in ends as work progresses.

Join with slip stitch as indicated unless otherwise stated.

SPECIAL STITCHES

Cluster (cl): Holding back last lp of each st on hook, 4 tr in indicated sp, yo and draw through all lps on hook.

Shell: (4 tr, ch 1, 4 tr) in place indicated

Large shell (lg shell): (4 tr, {ch 1, 4 tr} twice) in place indicated

4-back post treble decrease (4-bptr dec): Holding back last lp of each st on hook, **bptr** (see Stitch Guide) around each of next 4 sts, yo and draw through all lps on hook.

8-back post treble decrease (8-bptr dec): Holding back last lp of each st on hook, **bptr** (see Stitch Guide) around each of next 4 sts, sk sc between shells and working on next shell, bptr around each of next 4 sts, yo and draw through all lps on hook.

HOT PAD

Rnd 1: With A, ch 5, **join** (see Pattern Notes) in first ch to form ring, ch 1, [sc in ring, ch 5, **cl** (see Special Stitches) in ring, ch 5] 4 times, join in first sc. (4 cls, 4 sc, 8 ch-5 sps)

Rnd 2: Ch 1, sc in same sc as beg ch-1, ch 2, **lg shell** (see Special Stitches) in next cl, ch 2, sc in next sc, [ch 2, lg shell in next cl, ch 2, sc in next sc] 3 times, join in first sc. Fasten off. (4 lg shells, 4 sc, 8 ch-2 sps)

Rnd 3: Join B with sc in ch-1 sp of any shell, ch 5, **4-bptr dec** (see Special Stitches), ch 5, sc in ch-1 sp of next shell, ch 5, **8-bptr dec** (see Special Stitches), ch 5, [sc in ch-1 sp of next shell, ch 5, 4-bptr dec, ch 5, sc in ch-1 sp of next shell, ch 5, 8-bptr dec, ch 5] 3 times, join in first sc. (4 8-bptr dec, 4 4-bptr dec, 8 sc, 16 ch-5 sps)

Rnd 4: Ch 1, sc in same sc as beg ch-1, lg shell in top of next 4-bptr dec, sc in next sc, **shell** (see Special Stitches) in top of next 8-bptr dec, [sc in next sc, lg shell in top of next 4-bptr dec, sc in next sc, shell in top of next 8-bptr dec] 3 times, join in first sc. Fasten off. (4 lg shells, 4 shells, 8 sc)

Rnd 5: Join C with sc in first ch-1 sp of any lg shell, ch 5, 4-bptr dec, ch 5, sc in next ch-1 sp, ch 5, 8-bptr dec, ch 5, sc in ch-1 sp of next shell, ch 5, 8-bptr dec, ch 5, [sc in first ch-1 sp of next lg shell, ch 5, 4-bptr dec, ch 5, sc in next ch-1 sp, ch 5, 8-bptr dec, ch 5, sc in ch-1 sp of next shell, ch 5, 8-bptr dec, ch 5] 3 times, join in first sc. (8 8-bptr dec, 4 4-bptr dec, 12 sc, 24 ch-5 sps)

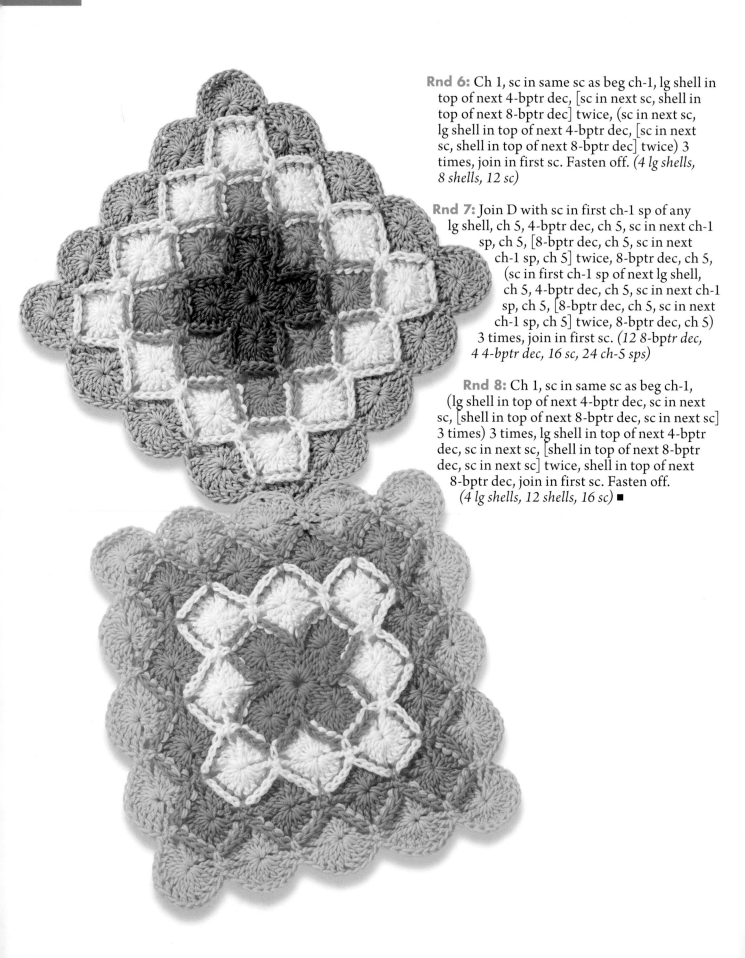

Rnd 6: Ch 1, sc in same sc as beg ch-1, lg shell in top of next 4-bptr dec, [sc in next sc, shell in top of next 8-bptr dec] twice, (sc in next sc, lg shell in top of next 4-bptr dec, [sc in next sc, shell in top of next 8-bptr dec] twice) 3 times, join in first sc. Fasten off. *(4 lg shells, 8 shells, 12 sc)*

Rnd 7: Join D with sc in first ch-1 sp of any lg shell, ch 5, 4-bptr dec, ch 5, sc in next ch-1 sp, ch 5, [8-bptr dec, ch 5, sc in next ch-1 sp, ch 5] twice, 8-bptr dec, ch 5, (sc in first ch-1 sp of next lg shell, ch 5, 4-bptr dec, ch 5, sc in next ch-1 sp, ch 5, [8-bptr dec, ch 5, sc in next ch-1 sp, ch 5] twice, 8-bptr dec, ch 5) 3 times, join in first sc. *(12 8-bptr dec, 4 4-bptr dec, 16 sc, 24 ch-5 sps)*

Rnd 8: Ch 1, sc in same sc as beg ch-1, (lg shell in top of next 4-bptr dec, sc in next sc, [shell in top of next 8-bptr dec, sc in next sc] 3 times) 3 times, lg shell in top of next 4-bptr dec, sc in next sc, [shell in top of next 8-bptr dec, sc in next sc] twice, shell in top of next 8-bptr dec, join in first sc. Fasten off. *(4 lg shells, 12 shells, 16 sc)* ■

Bag Holder

SKILL LEVEL

INTERMEDIATE

FINISHED SIZE
18 inches in circumference x 19 inches tall,
excluding handles

MATERIALS
- Omega Sinfonia light (light
  worsted) weight yarn (3½ oz/
  218 yds/100g per ball):
  1 ball each #879 purple (A), #828 lilac
  (B), #802 cream (C), #883 coral (D)
  and #834 gold (E)
- Size F/5/3.75mm crochet hook or size
  needed to obtain gauge
- Tapestry needle
- 7-inch length ¼-inch-wide elastic

GAUGE
2 shells and 3 sc = 4 inches

Take time to check gauge.

PATTERN NOTES
Weave in ends as work progresses.

Join with slip stitch as indicated unless otherwise stated.

Chain-4 at beginning of round counts as first
double crochet and chain-1 unless otherwise stated.

SPECIAL STITCHES

Shell: (4 tr, ch 1, 4 tr) in place indicated

8-back post treble decrease (8-bptr dec): Holding back last lp of each st on hook, bptr *(see Stitch Guide)* around each of next 4 sts, sk sc between shells and working on next shell, bptr around each of next 4 sts, yo and draw through all lps on hook.

BAG HOLDER

Rnd 1: With A, ch 80, **join** *(see Pattern Notes)* in first ch to form ring, **ch 4** *(see Pattern Notes),* sk next ch, *dc in next ch, ch 1, sk next ch, rep from * around, join in 3rd ch of beg ch-4. *(40 dc, 40 ch-1 sps)*

Rnd 2: Ch 1, sc in same ch as beg ch-1, *sk next 3 sts, **shell** *(see Special Stitches)* in next st, sk next 3 sts**, sc in next st, rep from * 9 times, ending last rep at **, join in first sc. Fasten off. *(10 shells, 10 sc)*

Rnd 3: Join B with sc in ch-1 sp of any shell, *ch 5, **8-bptr dec** *(see Special Stitches),* ch 5**, sc in ch-1 sp of next shell, rep from * 9 times, ending last rep at **, join in first sc. *(10 8-bptr dec, 10 sc, 20 ch-5 sps)*

Rnd 4: Ch 1, sc in same sc as beg ch-1, (shell in the top of next 8-bptr dec, sc in next sc) 9 times, shell in the top of next 8-bptr dec, join in first sc. Fasten off.

Rnds 5 & 6: With C, rep rnds 3 and 4.

Rnds 7 & 8: With D, rep rnds 3 and 4.

Rnds 9 & 10: With E, rep rnds 3 and 4.

Rnds 11 & 12: With A, rep rnds 3 and 4.

Rnds 13–22: Rep rnds 3–12.

Rnds 23–31: Rep rnds 3–11.

Rnd 32: Ch 4, sk next ch-1 sp, *dc in next st, ch 1, sk next ch-1 sp, rep from * around, join in 3rd ch of beg ch-4. *(40 dc, 40 ch-1 sps)*

Rnd 33: Ch 1, sc in each dc and each ch-1 sp around, join in first sc. *(80 sc)*

Rnd 34: Ch 1, sc in each of first 20 sc, ch 40 *(for handle)*, sk next 20 sc, sc in each of next 20 sc, ch 40 *(for handle)*, join in first sc. *(40 sc, 2 ch-40 sps)*

Rnd 35: Ch 1, sc in each sc and in each ch around, join in first sc. Fasten off. *(120 sc)*

CORD
Cut a 4¼-yd length of each color. Fold in half and knot loose ends. Place folded end over doorknob or hook. Put a pencil through other end and twist yarn until tight. Keeping strands taut, fold piece in half, allowing yarns to twist tog. Tie loose ends tog. Tie knot in opposite end of cord, trim ends to match.

FINISHING
Thread elastic through rnd 1, overlap ends and sew ends together.

Weave Cord through ch-1 sps of rnd 32. ∎

Purse

SKILL LEVEL

INTERMEDIATE

FINISHED SIZE

8 inches wide x 7 inches tall

MATERIALS

- Omega Sinfonia light (light worsted) weight yarn (3½ oz/218 yds/100g per ball):
    1 ball each #834 gold (A), #802 cream (B) and #821 mandarin (C)
- Size F/5/3.75mm crochet hook or size needed to obtain gauge
- Tapestry needle

GAUGE

4 sc = 1 inch

Take time to check gauge.

PATTERN NOTES

Weave in ends as work progresses.

Join with slip stitch as indicated unless otherwise stated.

SPECIAL STITCHES

Shell: (4 tr, ch 1, 4 tr) in place indicated

8-back post treble decrease (8-bptr dec): Holding back last lp of each st on hook, **bptr** *(see Stitch Guide)* around each of next 4 sts, sk sc between shells and working on next shell, bptr around each of next 4 sts, yo and draw through all lps on hook.

PURSE
BASE

Row 1: With A, ch 10, sc in 2nd ch from hook, sc in each rem ch across, turn. *(9 sc)*

Row 2: Ch 1, sc in each sc across, turn.

Rows 3–28: Rep row 2.

SIDES

Rnd 1: Now working in rnds, sc in first sc, sk next 3 sc, **shell** *(see Special Stitches)* in next sc, sk next 3 sc, sc in next sc, working across next side, sk first 4 rows, shell in end of next row, sk next 4 rows, sc in end of next row, sk next 4 rows, shell in end of next row, sk next 4 rows, sc in next row, sk next 4 rows, shell in end of next row, sk last 3 rows, working across next side in unused lps of foundation ch, sc in first ch, sk next 3 chs, shell in next ch, sk next 3 chs, sc in next ch, working across next side, sk first 4 rows, shell in end of next row, sk next 4 rows, sc in end of next row, sk next 4 rows, shell in end of next row, sk next 4 rows, sc in next row, sk next 4 rows, shell in end of next row, sk last 3 rows, **join** *(see Pattern Notes)* in first sc. *(8 shells, 8 sc)*

Rnd 2: Join B with sc in ch-1 sp of any shell, ch 5, **8-bptr dec** *(see Special Stitches)*, ch 5, [sc in ch-1 sp of next shell, ch 5, 8-bptr dec, ch 5] 7 times, join in first sc. *(8 8-bptr dec, 8 sc, 16 ch-1 sps)*

Rnd 3: Ch 1, sc in same sc as beg ch-1, shell in top of next 8-bptr dec, [sc in next sc, shell in top of next 8-bptr dec] 7 times, join in first sc. Fasten off.

Rnds 4 & 5: With C, rep rnds 2 and 3.

Rnds 6 & 7: With A, rep rnds 2 and 3.

Rnd 8: With B, rep rnd 2.

Rnd 9: Ch 1, sc in each st and in each ch around, join in **back lp** *(see Stitch Guide)* of first sc. *(64 sc)*

Rnd 10: Ch 1, sc in same lp as beg ch-1, working in back lp, sc in each rem sc around, join in back lp of first sc.

Rnd 11: Ch 1, sc in same lp as beg ch-1, working in back lp, sc in each of next 15 sc, ch 40 *(handle made)*, sk next 16 sc, sc in each of next 16 sc, ch 40 *(handle made)*, sk next 16 sc, join in back lp of first sc. *(32 sc, 2 ch-40 sps)*

Rnd 12: Ch 1, sc in same lp as beg ch-1, working in back lp, sc in each rem sc and in each ch around, join in first sc. Fasten off. ∎

Girl's Summer Hat

SKILL LEVEL

INTERMEDIATE

FINISHED SIZE
Fits 4–10 years

MATERIALS
- Omega Sinfonia light (light worsted) weight yarn (3½ oz/218 yds/100g per ball):
  1 ball each #802 cream (A), #828 lilac (B) and #879 purple (C)
- Size F/5/3.75mm crochet hook or size needed to obtain gauge
- Tapestry needle

GAUGE
2 shells and 3 sc = 4 inches

Take time to check gauge.

PATTERN NOTES
Weave in ends as work progresses.

Join with slip stitch as indicated unless otherwise stated.

Chain-5 at beginning of round counts as first double crochet and chain-2 unless otherwise stated.

SPECIAL STITCHES
Cluster (cl): Holding back last lp of each st on hook, 3 tr in indicated st, yo and draw through all 4 lps on hook.

Shell: (4 tr, ch 1, 4 tr) in place indicated

8-back post treble decrease (8-bptr dec): Holding back last lp of each st on hook, **bptr** (see Stitch Guide) around each of next 4 sts, sk sc between shells and working on next shell, bptr around each of next 4 sts, yo and draw through all lps on hook.

HAT
Rnd 1: Beg at top with A, ch 5, **join** (see Pattern Notes) in first ch to form ring, **ch 5** (see Pattern Notes), (dc in ring, ch 2) 7 times, join in 3rd ch of beg ch-5. (8 dc, 8 ch-2 sps)

Rnd 2: Ch 1, sc in same ch as beg ch-1, ch 5, **cl** (see Special Stitches) in next ch-2 sp, ch 5, [sc in next dc, ch 5, cl in next ch-2 sp, ch 5] 7 times, join in first sc. (8 cls, 8 sc, 16 ch-5 sps)

Rnd 3: Ch 1, sc in first sc, **shell** *(see Special Stitches)* in next cl, (sc in next sc, shell in next cl) 7 times, join in first sc. Fasten off. *(8 shells, 8 sc)*

Rnd 4: Join B with sc in ch-1 sp of any shell, ch 5, **8-bptr dec** *(see Special Stitches)*, ch 5, (sc in ch-1 sp of next shell, ch 5, 8-bptr dec, ch 5) 7 times, join in first sc. *(8 8-bptr dec, 8 sc, 16 ch-5 sps)*

Rnd 5: Ch 1, sc in same sc as beg ch-1, shell in top of next 8-bptr dec, (sc in next sc, shell in top of next 8-bptr dec) 7 times, join in first sc. Fasten off. *(8 shells, 8 sc)*

Rnds 6 & 7: With C, rep rnds 4 and 5.

Rnds 8 & 9: With A, rep rnds 4 and 5.

Rnds 10 & 11: With B, rep rnds 4 and 5.

Rnd 12: With C, rep rnd 4.

BRIM

Note: Brim is worked in continuous rnds. Do not join; mark beg of rnds.

Rnd 1: Ch 1, work 88 sc evenly sp around. **Do not join**.

Rnd 2: (2 sc in next st, sc in each of next 10 sts) 8 times. *(96 sc)*

Rnd 3: Sc in each sc around.

Rnd 4: (2 sc in next sc, sc in each of next 11 sc) 8 times. *(104 sc)*

Rnd 5: Rep rnd 3.

Rnd 6: (2 sc in next sc, sc in each of next 12 sc) 8 times. *(112 sc)*

Rnd 7: Rep rnd 3.

Rnd 8: (2 sc in next sc, sc in each of next 13 sc) 8 times *(120 sc)*

Rnd 9: Rep rnd 3.

Rnd 10: Sl st in each sc around, join in first sl st. Fasten off.

TIE
MAKE 1 OF EACH COLOR.
With one strand, ch 128. Fasten off.

FINISHING
Braid Ties together and tie knot in each end.
    Weave through rnd 12. Tie ends in bow. ∎

Baby Hat

SKILL LEVEL

INTERMEDIATE

FINISHED SIZES
Instructions given fit 6–12 months; changes for
1½–3 years are in [ ]

MATERIALS
- Omega Sinfonia light (light worsted)
  weight yarn (3½ oz/218 yds/100g
  per ball):
    1 ball each #802 cream (A), #828 lilac (B)
    and #879 purple (C)
- Size F/5/3.75mm crochet hook or size
  needed to obtain gauge
- Tapestry needle

GAUGE
2 shells and 3 sc = 4 inches

Take time to check gauge.

PATTERN NOTES
Weave in ends as work progresses.

Join with slip stitch as indicated unless otherwise stated.

Chain-5 at beginning of round counts as first
double crochet and chain-2 unless otherwise stated.

SPECIAL STITCHES
Cluster (cl): Holding back last lp of each st on
hook, 3 tr in indicated st, yo and draw through
all 4 lps on hook.

Shell: (4 tr, ch 1, 4 tr) in place indicated

8-back post treble decrease (8-bptr dec): Holding
back last lp of each st on hook, **bptr** *(see Stitch
Guide)* around each of next 4 sts, sk sc between
shells and working on next shell, bptr around
each of next 4 sts, yo and draw through all
lps on hook.

HAT
Rnd 1: Beg at top with A, ch 5, **join** *(see Pattern
Notes)* in first ch to form ring, **ch 5** *(see Pattern
Notes)*, (dc in ring, ch 2) 5 [6] times, join in
3rd ch of beg ch-5. *(6 [7] sc, 6 [7] ch-2 sps)*

Rnd 2: Ch 1, sc in same ch as beg ch-1, ch 5,
cl *(see Special Stitches)* in next ch-2 sp, ch 5,
(sc in next dc, ch 5, cl in next ch-2 sp, ch 5)
5 [6] times, join in first sc. *(6 [7] cls, 6 [7] sc,
12 [14] ch-5 sps)*

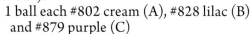

Rnd 3: Ch 1, sc in same sc as beg ch-1, **shell** (*see Special Stitches*) in next cl, (sc in next sc, shell in next cl) 5 [6] times, join in first sc. Fasten off. *(6 [7] shells, 6 [7] sc)*

Rnd 4: Join B with sc in ch-1 sp of any shell, ch 5, **8-bptr dec** (*see Special Stitches*), ch 5, [sc in ch-1 sp of next shell, ch 5, 8-bptr dec, ch 5] 5 [6] times, join in first sc. *(6 [7] 8-bptr dec, 6 [7] sc, 12 [14] ch-5 sps)*

Rnd 5: Ch 1, sc in same sc as beg ch-1, shell in top of next 8-bptr dec, [sc in next sc, shell in top of next 8-bptr dec] 5 [6] times, join in first sc. Fasten off. *(6 [7] shells, 6 [7] sc)*

Rnds 6 & 7: With C, rep rnds 4 and 5.

Rnds 8 & 9: With A, rep rnds 4 and 5.

Rnd 10: With B, rep rnd 4.

BRIM
Note: Brim is worked in continuous rnds. Do not join; mark beg of rnds.

Rnd 1: Ch 1, work 64 [72] sc evenly sp around. **Do not join.**

Rnd 2: (2 sc in next sc, sc in each of next 7 [8] sc) 8 times. *(72 [80] sc)*

Rnd 3: Sc in each sc around.

Rnd 4: (2 sc in next sc, sc in each of next 8 [9] sc) 8 times. *(80 [88] sc)*

Rnd 5: Rep rnd 3.

Rnd 6: (2 sc in next sc, sc in each of next 9 [10] sc) 8 times. *(88 [96] sc)*

Rnd 7: Rep rnd 3.

FOR 6–12 MONTH SIZE
Rnd 8: Ch 1, sl st in each sc around, join in joining sl st. Fasten off.

FOR 1½–3 YEAR SIZE
Rnd 8: (2 sc in next sc, sc in each of next 11 sc) 8 times. *([104] sc)*

Rnd 9: Rep rnd 3.

Rnd 10: Ch 1, sl st in each sc around, join in joining sl st. Fasten off. ∎

Baby Booties

SKILL LEVEL

INTERMEDIATE

FINISHED SIZES

Instructions given fit newborn–3 months; changes for 3–6 months and 6–12 months are in [ ].

MATERIALS

- Crystal Palace Mini-Mochi super fine (sock) weight yarn (1¾ oz/ 195 yds/50g per ball):
  1 ball #103 violets rainbow
- Size B/1/2.25mm crochet hook or size needed to obtain gauge
- Tapestry needle
- 4 stitch markers

1 SUPER FINE

GAUGE

13 sc and 14 rnds = 2 inches

Take time to check gauge.

PATTERN NOTES

Weave in ends as work progresses.

Join with slip stitch as indicated unless otherwise stated.

SPECIAL STITCHES

Shell: (4 tr, ch 1, 4 tr) in place indicated

8-back post treble decrease (8-bptr dec): Holding back last lp of each st on hook, **bptr** (*see Stitch Guide*) around each of next 4 sts, sk sc between shells and working on next shell, bptr around each of next 4 sts, yo and draw through all lps on hook.

BOOTIE
MAKE 2.

*Note: Bootie is worked in continuous rnds.
Do not join; mark beg of rnds.*

Rnd 1 (RS): Ch 9 [9, 11], 3 sc in 2nd ch from hook, sc in each of next 6 [6, 8] chs, 3 sc in last ch, working in unused lps on opposite side of foundation ch, sc in each of next 6 [6, 8] chs. **Do not join.** (*18 [18, 22] sc*)

Note: Place marker in 2nd sc of each 3-sc group. Move markers up as work progresses.

Rnd 2: Sc in each sc around.

Rnd 3: Sc in each st to next marked sc, 3 sc in marked sc (*mark 2nd sc*), sc in each sc to next marked sc, 3 sc in marked sc (*mark 2nd sc*), sc in each rem sc. (*22 [22, 26] sc*)

Rnd 4: Sc in each sc around.

Rnds 5–8 [5–10, 5–16]: [Rep rnds 3 and 4 alternately] 2 [3, 6] times. (*30 [34, 50] sc at end of last rnd*)

Note: *Check width at end of last rnd. Laid flat, width should be 2 [2½, 3] inches. If not, change to a smaller or larger hook.*

Rnds 9–14 [11–19, 17–21]: Rep rnd 2.

Note: *Mark center 8 [8, 12] sc on one side between side markers. Remove side markers.*

Row 1: Now working in rows, sc in each of next 4 [5, 7] sc, leaving rem sts unworked, turn. (*4, 5, 7] sc*)

Row 2: Ch 1, sc in each of first 22 [26, 38] sc, leaving rem sts unworked, turn. (*22 [26, 38] sc*)

Row 3: Ch 1, sc in each sc across, turn.

Rows 4–11 [4–11, 4–14]: Rep row 2.

Fold piece in half and sl st through both thicknesses to form heel seam. Fasten off.

EDGING
Rnd 1: With RS facing, **join** (*see Pattern Notes*) yarn in heel seam, work (**shell** (*see Special Stitches*), sc) 5 times evenly sp (*about 1-inch apart*) around ankle opening. **Do not join.** (*5 shells, 5 sc*)

Rnd 2: Sl st in each of next 4 sts and in next ch-1 sp, ch 1, sc in same sp as beg ch-1, ch 5, **8-bptr dec** (*see Special Stitches*), ch 5, (sc in ch-1 sp of next shell, ch 5, 8-bptr dec, ch 5) 4 times, join in first sc. (*30 [34, 50] sc at end of last rnd*)

Rnd 3: Ch 1, sc in same sc as beg ch-1, shell in top of next 8-bptr dec, (sc in next sc, shell in top of next 8-bptr dec) 4 times, join in first sc. (*5 shells, 5 sc*)

Rnd 4: Sl st in each of next 3 sts and in next ch-1 sp, ch 1, sc in same sp as beg ch-1, ch 5, 8-bptr dec, ch 5, (sc in ch-1 sp of next shell, ch 5, 8-dec, ch 5) 4 times, join in first sc. Fasten off. ∎

Ladies
Slippers

SKILL LEVEL

INTERMEDIATE

SIZES

Instructions given fit adult small; changes for medium and large are in [ ].

FINISHED SIZES

8-inch sole (*small*) [9-inch sole (*medium*), 10-inch sole (*large*)]

MATERIALS

- Plymouth Dreambaby DK light (light worsted) weight yarn (1¾ oz/183 yds/50g per ball):
  2 balls #143 lima bean (A)
  1 ball each #0305 happy spots (B) and #142 egg cream (C)
- Size F/5/3.75mm and G/6/4mm crochet hooks or size needed to obtain gauge
- Tapestry needle
- 4 stitch markers

GAUGE

With size G hook: 8 sc and 11 rnds = 2 inches

Take time to check gauge.

PATTERN NOTES

Weave in ends as work progresses.

Join with slip stitch as indicated unless otherwise stated.

SPECIAL STITCHES

Shell: (4 tr, ch 1, 4 tr) in place indicated

8-back post treble decrease (8-bptr dec): Holding back last lp of each st on hook, **bptr** (*see Stitch Guide*) around each of next 4 sts, sk sc between shells and working on next shell, bptr around each of next 4 sts, yo and draw through all lps on hook.

SLIPPER
MAKE 2.

Note: Slipper is worked in continuous rnds. Do not join; mark beg of rnds.

Rnd 1 (RS): Beg at toe with size G hook and A, ch 9 [9, 11], 3 sc in 2nd ch from hook, sc in each of next 6 [6, 8] chs, 3 sc in last ch, working in unused lps on opposite side of foundation ch, sc in each of next 6 [6, 8] chs. **Do not join.** *(18 [18, 22] sc)*

Note: Place marker in 2nd sc of each 3-sc group. Move markers up as work progresses.

Rnd 2: Sc in each sc around.

Rnd 3: Sc in each st to next marked sc, 3 sc in marked sc *(mark 2nd sc)*, sc in each sc to next marked sc, 3 sc in marked sc *(mark 2nd sc)*, sc in each rem sc. *(22 [22, 26] sc)*

Rnds 4–8 [4–10, 4–16]: [Rep rnds 2 and 3 alternately] 3 [3, 6] times. *(30 [34, 50] sc at end of last rnd)*

Note: Check width at end of last rnd. Laid flat, width should be 3½ [4¼, 5] inches. If not, change to a smaller or larger hook.

Rnds 9–27 [11–29, 17–31]: Rep rnd 2.

Note: Mark center 8 [8, 12] sc on one side between side markers. Remove side markers.

Row 1: Now working in rows, sc in each of next 4 [5, 9] sc, leaving rem sts unworked, turn. *(4 [5, 9] sc)*

Row 2: Ch 1, sc in each of first 22 [26, 38] sc, leaving rem sts unworked, turn. *(22 [26, 38] sc)*

Row 3: Ch 1, sc in each sc across, turn.

Rows 4–18 [4–20, 4–24]: Rep row 3.

Fold piece in half and sl st through both thicknesses to form heel seam. Fasten off.

EDGING

Rnd 1: With RS facing and size F hook, join A with sc in heel seam, work 47 sc evenly sp around ankle opening. **Do not join.** *(48 sc)*

Rnd 2: Working in **back lp** *(see Stitch Guide)*, sc in each sc around. **Do not join.**

Rnd 3: Ch 1, sc in next sc, sk next 3 sc, **shell** *(see Special Stitches)* in next sc, (sk next 3 sc, sc in next sc, sk next 3 sc, shell in the next sc) 5 times, sk next 3 sc, **join** *(see Pattern Notes)* in first sc. Fasten off. *(6 shells, 6 sc)*

Rnd 4: Join B with sc in ch-1 sp of any shell, ch 5, **8-bptr dec** *(see Special Stitches)*, ch 5, (sc in ch-1 sp of next shell, ch 5, 8-bptr dec, ch 5) 5 times, join in first sc. *(6 8-bptr dec, 6 sc, 12 ch-5 sps)*

Rnd 5: Ch 1, sc in first sc, shell in top of next 8-bptr dec, (sc in next sc, shell in top of next 8-bptr dec) 5 times, join in first sc. Fasten off. *(6 shells, 6 sc)*

Rnd 6 & 7: With C, rep rnds 4 and 5.

Rnds 8 & 9: With A, rep rnds 4 and 5. At end of rnd 9, do not fasten off.

Rnd 10: Ch 1, sl st in each st around, join in joining sl st. Fasten off. ■

Slouchy Beanie

SKILL LEVEL

INTERMEDIATE

FINISHED SIZE
Fits 21-inch head circumference

MATERIALS
- Plymouth Encore DK light (light worsted) weight yarn (1¾ oz/ 150 yds/50g per ball):
  2 balls #240 taupe
- Size F/5/3.75mm crochet hook or size needed to obtain gauge
- Tapestry needle

GAUGE
2 shells and 3 sc = 4 inches

Take time to check gauge.

PATTERN NOTES
Weave in ends as work progresses.

Join with slip stitch as indicated unless otherwise stated.

SPECIAL STITCHES
Shell: (4 tr, ch 1, 4 tr) in place indicated.

8-back post treble decrease (8-bptr dec): Holding back last lp of each st on hook, **bptr** (*see Stitch Guide*) around each of next 4 sts, sk sc between shells and working on next shell, bptr around each of next 4 sts, yo and draw through all lps on hook.

BEANIE
Rnd 1: Ch 80, **join** (*see Pattern Notes*) in first ch to form ring, ch 1, sc in same ch as beg ch-1, sk next 3 chs, **shell** (*see Special Stitches*) in next ch, sk next 3 chs, [sc in next ch, sk next 3 chs, shell in next ch, sk next 3 chs] 9 times, join in first sc. (*10 shells, 10 sc*)

Rnd 2: Sl st in each of next 4 sts, ch 1, sc in next ch-1 sp, ch 5, **8-bptr dec** (*see Special Stitches*), ch 5, [sc in ch-1 sp of next shell, 8-bptr dec, ch 5] 9 times, join in first sc. (*10 8-bptr dec, 10 sc, 20 ch-5 sps*)

Rnd 3: Ch 1, sc in same sc as beg ch-1, shell in top of next 8-bptr dec, [sc in next sc, shell in top of next 8-bptr dec] 9 times, join in first sc. (*10 shells, 10 sc*)

Rep rnds 2 and 3 until piece measures 11 inches from beg. At end of last rnd, fasten off, leaving a 12-inch end.

FINISHING
With tapestry needle, weave end through ch-1 sps of last rnd. Gather to close opening and secure end. ■

Fingerless Gloves
& Beanie

FINGERLESS GLOVES

SKILL LEVEL

INTERMEDIATE

FINISHED SIZE
7½ inches long x 8 inches in circumference

MATERIALS
- Kollage Riveting Sport fine (sport) weight yarn (3½ oz/350 yds/100g per ball):
  1 ball each #7902 dusk denim (A), #7904 charcoal denim (B) and #7906 cloud denim (C)
- Sizes E/4/3.5mm and F/5/3.75mm crochet hooks or size needed to obtain gauge
- Tapestry needle

GAUGE
With size F hook: 2 shells and 3 sc = 4 inches

Take time to check gauge.

PATTERN NOTES
Weave in ends as work progresses.

Join with slip stitch as indicated unless otherwise stated.

SPECIAL STITCHES
Shell: (4 tr, ch 1, 4 tr) in place indicated

8-back post treble decrease (8-bptr dec): Holding back last lp of each st on hook, **bptr** (see Stitch Guide) around each of next 4 sts, sk sc between shells and working on next shell, bptr around each of next 4 sts, yo and draw through all lps on hook.

FINGERLESS GLOVES
MAKE 2.

Rnd 1: Beg at wrist with A, ch 40, **join** (see Pattern Notes) in first ch to form ring, ch 1, sc in same ch as joining, sk next 3 chs, **shell** (see Special Stitches) in next ch, sk next 3 chs, (sc in next ch, sk next 3 chs, shell in next ch, sk next 3 chs) 4 times, join in first sc. Fasten off. (5 shells, 5 sc)

Rnd 2: Join B with sc in ch-1 sp of any shell, ch 1, sc in same sp as beg ch-1, ch 5, **8-bptr dec** (see Special Stitches, ch 5, (sc in ch-1 sp of next shell, ch 5, 8-bptr dec, ch 5) 4 times, join in first sc. (5 8-bptr dec, 5 sc, 10 ch-5 sps)

Rnd 3: Ch 1, sc in same sc as beg ch-1, shell in top of next 8-bptr dec, (sc in next sc, shell in top of next 8-bptr dec) 4 times, join in first sc. Fasten off. (5 shells, 10 sc)

Rnds 4 & 5: With C, rep rnds 2 and 3.

Rnds 6 & 7: With A, rep rnds 2 and 3.

Rnds 8–11: Rep rnds 2–5.

Rnd 12: Join A with sc in ch-1 sp of any shell, ch 5, 8-bptr dec, ch 5, (sc in ch-1 sp of next shell, ch 5, 8-bptr dec, ch 5) 3 times, sc in ch-1 sp of next shell, ch 11 (thumb opening), join in first sc. (5 8-bptr dec, 5 sc, 8 ch-5 sps, 1 ch-11 sp)

Rnd 13: Ch 1, sc in same sc as beg ch-1, (shell in top of next 8-bptr dec, sc in next sc) 4 times, sk next 5 chs, shell in next ch, sk next 5 chs, join in first sc. Fasten off. (5 shells, 5 sc)

Rnds 14 & 15: With B, rep rnds 2 and 3. At end of rnd 15, do not fasten off.

Rnd 16: Sl st in each st around, join in joining sl st. Fasten off.

THUMB EDGING

Note: Thumb edging is worked in continuous rnds. Do not join unless specified; mark beg of rnds.

Rnd 1 (RS): With size E hook, join B in bottom of thumb opening, ch 1, work 20 sc evenly sp around opening. **Do not join.**

Rnd 2: Sc in **back lp** *(see Stitch Guide)* of each sc around.

Rnds 3–5: Rep rnd 2. At end of last rnd, fasten off.

BEANIE

SKILL LEVEL

INTERMEDIATE

FINISHED SIZE
Fits 21-inch head circumference

MATERIALS
- Kollage Riveting Sport fine (sport) weight yarn (3½ oz/350 yds/100g per ball):
    1 ball each #7902 dusk denim (A), #7904 charcoal denim (B) and #7906 cloud denim (C)
- Size G/6/4mm crochet hook or size needed to obtain gauge
- Tapestry needle

GAUGE
2 shells and 3 sc = 4 inches

Take time to check gauge.

PATTERN NOTES
Weave in ends as work progresses.

Join with slip stitch as indicated unless otherwise stated.

SPECIAL STITCHES
Shell: (4 tr, ch 1, 4 tr) in place indicated

8-back post treble decrease (8-bptr dec): Holding back last lp of each st on hook, **bptr** *(see Stitch Guide)* around each of next 4 sts, sk sc between shells and working on next shell, bptr around each of next 4 sts, yo and draw through all lps on hook.

BEANIE
Rnd 1: With A, ch 80, **join** *(see Pattern Notes)* in first ch to form ring, ch 1, sc in same ch as joining, sk next 3 chs, **shell** *(see Special Stitches)* in next ch, sk next 3 chs, sc in next ch, (sc in next ch, sk next 3 chs, shell in next ch, sk next 3 chs, sc in next ch) 9 times, join in first sc. Fasten off. *(10 shells, 20 sc)*

Rnd 2: Join B with sc in ch-1 sp of any shell, ch 5, **8-bptr dec** *(see Special Stitches)*, ch 5, (sc in ch-1 sp of next shell, ch 5, 8-bptr dec, ch 5) 9 times, join in first sc. *(10 8-bptr dec, 10 sc, 20 ch-5 sps)*

Rnd 3: Ch 1, sc in same sc as beg ch-1, shell in top of next 8-bptr dec, (sc in next sc, shell in top of next 8-bptr dec) 9 times, join in first sc. Fasten off. *(10 shells, 10 sc)*

Rnds 4 & 5: With C, rep rnds 2 and 3.

Rnds 6 & 7: With A, rep rnds 2 and 3.

Rnds 8–19: [Rep rnds 2–7] twice.

Rnds 20 & 21: With A, rep rnds 2 and 3. At end of rnd 21, fasten off, leaving a 12-inch end.

FINISHING

With tapestry needle, weave end through ch-1 sp of first shell on rnd 21, weave through ch-1 sps of rem shells. Gather to close opening and secure end. ∎

Cowl

SKILL LEVEL

INTERMEDIATE

FINISHED SIZE
14 inches wide x 42 inches in circumference

MATERIALS
- Filatura Di Crosa Charly bulky (chunky) weight yarn (1¾ oz/ 71 yds/50g per ball): 3 balls each #1162 sand (A), #1669 taupe heather (B) and #1683 chestnut heather
- Size J/10/6mm crochet hook or size needed to obtain gauge
- Tapestry needle

5 BULKY

GAUGE
1½ shells = 4 inches

Take time to check gauge.

PATTERN NOTES
Weave in ends as work progresses.

Join with slip stitch as indicated unless otherwise stated.

SPECIAL STITCHES
Shell: (4 tr, ch 1, 4 tr) in place indicated.

8-back post treble decrease (8-bptr dec): Holding back last lp of each st on hook, **bptr** (see Stitch Guide) around each of next 4 sts, sk sc between shells and working on next shell, bptr around each of next 4 sts, yo and draw through all lps on hook.

COWL
Rnd 1: With A, ch 128, **join** (see Pattern Notes) in first ch to form ring, ch 1, sc in same ch as joining, sk next 3 chs, **shell** (see Special Stitches) in next ch, sk next 3 chs, sc in next ch, [sc in next ch, sk next 3 chs, shell in next ch, sk next 3 chs, sc in next ch] 15 times, join in first sc. Fasten off. *(16 shells, 32 sc)*

Rnd 2: Join B with sc in any ch-1 sp, ch 5, **8-bptr dec** (see Special Stitches), ch 5, [sc in ch-1 sp of next shell, ch 5, 8-bptr dec, ch 5] 14 times, join in first sc. *(16 8-bptr dec, 16 sc, 32 ch-5 sps)*

Rnd 3: Ch 1, sc in same sc as beg ch-1, shell in the top of next 8-bptr dec, [sc in next sc, shell in the top of next 8-bptr dec] 15 times, join in first sc. Fasten off. *(16 shells, 16 sc)*

Rnds 4 & 5: With C, rep rnds 2 and 3.

Rnds 6 & 7: With A, rep rnds 2 and 3.

Rnds 8 & 9: With B, rep rnds 2 and 3.

Rnds 10–15: Rep rnds 4–9.

Rnds 16–18: Rep rnds 4–6. At end of rnd 18, fasten off. ∎

Bottle Cover

SKILL LEVEL

INTERMEDIATE

FINISHED SIZE
9 inches in circumference x 9 inches tall

MATERIALS
- Kollage Riveting Worsted medium (worsted) weight yarn (3½ oz/ 163 yds/100g per ball):
  1 ball each #8104 charcoal denim (A), #8102 dusk denim (B) and #8106 cloud denim (C)
- Size G/6/4mm crochet hook or size needed to obtain gauge
- Tapestry needle
- Toggle closure

GAUGE
1½ shells = 4 inches

Take time to check gauge.

PATTERN NOTES
Weave in ends as work progresses.

Join with slip stitch as indicated unless otherwise stated.

SPECIAL STITCHES
Shell: (4 tr, ch 1, 4 tr) in place indicated

8-back post treble decrease (8-bptr dec): Holding back last lp of each st on hook, **bptr** (*see Stitch Guide*) around each of next 4 sts, sk sc between shells and working on next shell, bptr around each of next 4 sts, yo and draw through all lps on hook.

BOTTLE COVER
BASE

Rnd 1: With A, ch 5, **join** *(see Pattern Notes)* in first ch to form ring, ch 1, 10 sc in ring. Do not join. *(10 sc)*

Rnd 2: 2 sc in each sc around. *(20 sc)*

Rnd 3: Sc in each sc around.

Rnd 4: (2 sc in next sc, sc in next sc) 10 times. *(30 sc)*

Rnd 5: Rep rnd 3.

Rnd 6: (2 sc in next sc, sc in each of next 2 sc) 10 times. *(40 sc)*

Rnd 7: Rep rnd 3.

BODY

Rnd 8: Ch 1, sc in same sc as beg ch-1, [sk next 3 sc, **shell** *(see Special Stitches)* in next sc, sk next 3 sc, sc in next sc] 5 times, join in first sc. Fasten off. *(5 shells, 5 sc)*

Rnd 9: Join B with sc in ch-1 sp of any shell, ch 5, **8-bptr dec** *(see Special Stitches)*, ch 5, [sc in ch-1 sp of next shell, 8-bptr dec, ch 5] 4 times, join in first sc. *(5 8-bptr dec, 5 sc, 10 ch-5 sps)*

Rnd 10: Ch 1, sc in same sc as beg ch-1, shell in the top of next 8-bptr dec, (sc in next sc, shell in top of next 8-bptr dec) 5 times, join in first sc. Fasten off. *(5 shells, 5 sc)*

Rnds 11 & 12: With C, rep rnds 9 and 10.

Rnds 13 & 14: With A, rep rnds 2 and 3.

Rnds 15–20: Rep rnds 9–14.

CORD

With 2 strands of A held tog, ch 90. Fasten off.

FINISHING

Weave Cord through ch-1 sps of rnd 20. Thread Cord ends through toggle and tie a knot at each end. To secure toggle, tie knot above knotted ends. ■

Mug Wraps

SKILL LEVEL

INTERMEDIATE

FINISHED SIZES

Small mug wrap: 3½ inches wide x 8 inches in circumference

Large mug wrap: 5½ inches wide x 8 inches in circumference

MATERIALS

Small Mug Wrap
- Plymouth Encore DK light (light worsted) weight yarn (1¾ oz/150 yds/ 50g per ball):
   1 ball each #1444 dark brown heather (A) and #256 ecru (B)
- Size E/4/3.5mm crochet hook or size needed to obtain gauge
- Tapestry needle

Large Mug Wrap
- Plymouth Encore DK light (light worsted) weight yarn (1¾ oz/150 yds/ 50g per ball):
   1 ball each #240 taupe (A), #256 ecru (B) and #1444 dark brown heather (C)
- Sizes E/4/3.5mm and F/5/3.75mm crochet hooks or size needed to obtain gauge
- Tapestry needle

GAUGE

With size F hook: 2 shells and 3 sc = 4 inches

Take time to check gauge.

PATTERN NOTES

Weave in ends as work progresses.

Join with slip stitch as indicated unless otherwise stated.

SPECIAL STITCHES

Shell: (4 tr, ch 1, 4 tr) in place indicated

8-back post treble decrease (8-bptr dec): Holding back last lp of each st on hook, **bptr** (*see Stitch Guide*) around each of next 4 sts, sk sc between shells and working on next shell, bptr around each of next 4 sts, yo and draw through all lps on hook.

SMALL MUG WRAP

Rnd 1: With size E hook and A, ch 40, **join** (*see Pattern Notes*) in first ch to form ring, ch 1, sc in same ch as joining, sk next 4 chs, **shell** (*see Special Stitches*) in next ch, sk next 4 chs, [sc in next ch, sk next 4 chs, shell in next ch, sk next 4 chs] 3 times, join in 3rd ch of beg ch-4. Fasten off. (*4 shells, 4 sc*)

Rnd 2: Join B with sc in ch-1 sp of any shell, ch 5, **8-bptr dec** (*see Special Stitches*), ch 5, [sc in ch-1 sp of next shell, ch 5, 8-bptr dec, ch 5] 3 times, join in first sc. (*4 8-bptr dec, 4 sc, 8 ch-5 sps*)

Rnd 3: Ch 1, sc in same sc as beg ch-1, shell in top of next 8-bptr dec, [sc in next sc, 8-bptr dec] 3 times, join in first sc. Fasten off. (*4 shells, 4 sc*)

Rnds 4 & 5: With A, rep rnds 2 and 3.

BOTTOM EDGING

Hold piece with foundation ch at top, join A with sc in unused lp of ch at bottom of first sc, shell in unused lp of ch at bottom of next shell, [sc in unused lp of ch at bottom of next sc, shell in unused lp of ch at bottom of next shell] 3 times, join in first sc. Fasten off. (*4 shells, 4 sc*)

LARGE MUG WRAP

Rnd 1: With size E hook and A, ch 32, **join** (*see Pattern Notes*) in first ch to form ring, ch 1, sc in same ch as joining, sk next 3 chs, **shell** (*see Special Stitches*) in next ch, sk next 3 chs, [sc in next ch, sk next 3 chs, shell in next ch, sk next 3 chs] 3 times, join in 3rd ch of beg ch-4. Fasten off. (*4 shells*)

Rnd 2: Join B with sc in ch-1 sp of any shell, ch 5, **8-bptr dec** (*see Special Stitches*), ch 5, [sc in ch-1 sp of next shell, ch 5, 8-bptr dec, ch 5] 3 times, join in first sc. (*4 8-bptr dec, 4 sc, 8 ch-5 sps*)

Rnd 3: Ch 1, sc in same sc as beg ch-1, shell in top of next 8-bptr dec, [sc in next sc, shell in top of next 8-bptr dec] 3 times, join in first sc. Fasten off. (*4 shells, 4 sc*)

Rnds 4 & 5: With size F hook and C, rep rnds 2 and 3.

Rnds 6 & 7: With size F hook and A, rep rnds 2 and 3.

Rnds 8 & 9: With size F hook and B, rep rnds 2 and 3.

Rnd 10: Ch 1, sl st in each st around, join in joining sl st. Fasten off. ∎

STITCH GUIDE

FOR MORE COMPLETE INFORMATION,
VISIT **ANNIESCATALOG.COM/STITCHGUIDE**

STITCH ABBREVIATIONS

beg . . . . begin/begins/beginning
bpdc . . . . back post double crochet
bpsc . . . . .back post single crochet
bptr . . . . .back post treble crochet
CC . . . . contrasting color
ch(s) . . . . .chain(s)
ch- . . . . refers to chain or space
previously made (i.e., ch-1 space)
ch sp(s) . . . . chain space(s)
cl(s) . . . . cluster(s)
cm . . . . centimeter(s)
dc . . . . double crochet (singular/plural)
dc dec . . . . double crochet 2 or more
stitches together, as indicated
dec . . . . decrease/decreases/decreasing
dtr . . . . double treble crochet
ext . . . . .extended
fpdc . . . . front post double crochet
fpsc . . . . front post single crochet
fptr . . . . front post treble crochet
g . . . . .gram(s)
hdc . . . . half double crochet
hdc dec . . . . half double crochet 2 or more
stitches together, as indicated
inc . . . . increase/increases/increasing
lp(s) . . . . .loop(s)
MC . . . . .main color
mm . . . . millimeter(s)
oz . . . . .ounce(s)
pc . . . . popcorn(s)
rem . . . . remain/remains/remaining
rep(s) . . . . .repeat(s)
rnd(s) . . . . round(s)
RS . . . . right side
sc . . . . single crochet (singular/plural)
sc dec . . . . .single crochet 2 or more
stitches together, as indicated
sk . . . . .skip/skipped/skipping
sl st(s) . . . . slip stitch(es)
sp(s) . . . . space(s)/spaced
st(s) . . . . stitch(es)
tog . . . . .together
tr . . . . treble crochet
trtr . . . . .triple treble
WS . . . . wrong side
yd(s) . . . . .yard(s)
yo . . . . yarn over

YARN CONVERSION

OUNCES TO GRAMS	GRAMS TO OUNCES
1 . . . . 28.4	25 . . . . ⅞
2 . . . . 56.7	40 . . . . 1⅔
3 . . . . 85.0	50 . . . . 1¾
4 . . . . 113.4	100 . . . . 3½

UNITED STATES		UNITED KINGDOM
sl st (slip stitch)	=	sc (single crochet)
sc (single crochet)	=	dc (double crochet)
hdc (half double crochet)	=	htr (half treble crochet)
dc (double crochet)	=	tr (treble crochet)
tr (treble crochet)	=	dtr (double treble crochet)
dtr (double treble crochet)	=	ttr (triple treble crochet)
skip	=	miss

Single crochet decrease (sc dec): (Insert hook, yo, draw lp through) in each of the sts indicated, yo, draw through all lps on hook.

Example of 2-sc dec

Half double crochet decrease (hdc dec): (Yo, insert hook, yo, draw lp through) in each of the sts indicated, yo, draw through all lps on hook.

Example of 2-hdc dec

Double crochet decrease (dc dec): (Yo, insert hook, yo, draw lp through, yo, draw through 2 lps on hook) in each of the sts indicated, yo, draw through all lps on hook.

Example of 2-dc dec

Treble crochet decrease (tr dec): Holding back last lp of each st, tr in each of the sts indicated, yo, pull through all lps on hook.

Example of 2-tr dec

Reverse single crochet (reverse sc): Ch 1, sk first st, working from left to right, insert hook in next st from front to back, draw up lp on hook, yo and draw through both lps on hook.

Chain (ch): Yo, pull through lp on hook.

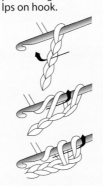

Single crochet (sc): Insert hook in st, yo, pull through st, yo, pull through both lps on hook.

Double crochet (dc): Yo, insert hook in st, yo, pull through st, [yo, pull through 2 lps] twice.

Front loop (front lp) Back loop (back lp)

Front Loop   Back Loop

Front post stitch (fp): Back post stitch (bp): When working post st, insert hook from right to left around post of st on previous row.

Back   Front

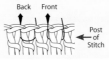

Post of Stitch

Half double crochet (hdc): Yo, insert hook in st, yo, pull through st, yo, pull through all 3 lps on hook.

Double treble crochet (dtr): Yo 3 times, insert hook in st, yo, pull through st, [yo, pull through 2 lps] 4 times.

Slip stitch (sl st): Insert hook in st, pull through both lps on hook.

Chain color change (ch color change) Yo with new color, draw through last lp on hook.

Double crochet color change (dc color change) Drop first color, yo with new color, draw through last 2 lps of st.

Treble crochet (tr): Yo twice, insert hook in st, yo, pull through st, [yo, pull through 2 lps] 3 times.

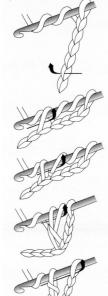

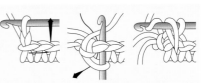

Metric
Conversion
Charts

METRIC CONVERSIONS

yards	x	.9144	=	metres (m)
yards	x	91.44	=	centimetres (cm)
inches	x	2.54	=	centimetres (cm)
inches	x	25.40	=	millimetres (mm)
inches	x	.0254	=	metres (m)

centimetres	x	.3937	=	inches
metres	x	1.0936	=	yards

INCHES INTO MILLIMETRES & CENTIMETRES (Rounded off slightly)

inches	mm	cm	inches	cm	inches	cm	inches	cm
1/8	3	0.3	5	12.5	21	53.5	38	96.5
1/4	6	0.6	5 1/2	14	22	56	39	99
3/8	10	1	6	15	23	58.5	40	101.5
1/2	13	1.3	7	18	24	61	41	104
5/8	15	1.5	8	20.5	25	63.5	42	106.5
3/4	20	2	9	23	26	66	43	109
7/8	22	2.2	10	25.5	27	68.5	44	112
1	25	2.5	11	28	28	71	45	114.5
1 1/4	32	3.2	12	30.5	29	73.5	46	117
1 1/2	38	3.8	13	33	30	76	47	119.5
1 3/4	45	4.5	14	35.5	31	79	48	122
2	50	5	15	38	32	81.5	49	124.5
2 1/2	65	6.5	16	40.5	33	84	50	127
3	75	7.5	17	43	34	86.5		
3 1/2	90	9	18	46	35	89		
4	100	10	19	48.5	36	91.5		
4 1/2	115	11.5	20	51	37	94		

KNITTING NEEDLES CONVERSION CHART

Canada/U.S.	0	1	2	3	4	5	6	7	8	9	10	10½	11	13	15
Metric (mm)	2	2¼	2¾	3¼	3½	3¾	4	4½	5	5½	6	6½	8	9	10

CROCHET HOOKS CONVERSION CHART

Canada/U.S.	1/B	2/C	3/D	4/E	5/F	6/G	8/H	9/I	10/J	10½/K	N
Metric (mm)	2.25	2.75	3.25	3.5	3.75	4.25	5	5.5	6	6.5	9.0

Annie's® *Bavarian Crochet on-the-Go* is published by Annie's, 306 East Parr Road, Berne, IN 46711. Printed in USA. Copyright © 2013 Annie's. All rights reserved. This publication may not be reproduced in part or in whole without written permission from the publisher.

RETAIL STORES: If you would like to carry this pattern book or any other Annie's publications, visit AnniesWSL.com.

Every effort has been made to ensure that the instructions in this pattern book are complete and accurate. We cannot, however, take responsibility for human error, typographical mistakes or variations in individual work. Please visit AnniesCustomerCare.com to check for pattern updates.

ISBN: 978-1-59635-780-8
3 4 5 6 7 8 9